Viewing the Holocaust Today

Philip Brooks

Heinemann Library
Chicago, Illinois

Introduction

What Was the Holocaust?

The Holocaust is the name given to the systematic persecution and murder of approximately six million Jewish people in Europe between 1939 and 1945. Germany's **Nazi** government carried out these crimes, sometimes with the aid, voluntary or involuntary, of government officials and citizens in other European countries.

The Holocaust began in Germany at the start of World War II. As Germany's armies swept across Poland, France, Holland, and beyond, they brought the destruction of Jewish communities. By 1945, six million of Europe's estimated nine million Jews were dead.

The Nazis also targeted other groups for mistreatment. Approximately 200,000 mentally and physically disabled people were killed. **Gypsies,** Poles, Russians, political enemies of the Nazi regime, homosexuals, and **Jehovah's Witnesses** were among the groups persecuted and in many cases murdered along with European Jews. During the war, German forces were also responsible for the deaths of three million Soviet **prisoners of war,** killed by starvation, exposure, beatings, and shootings.

Why Did it Happen?

Following its 1918 defeat in World War I, Germany experienced economic troubles. The Treaty of Paris that ended the war left Germany bankrupt and isolated. Ordinary Germans were going hungry and those who were better off grew tired of worrying about their country's future. So, when a strong-voiced, self-confident politician named Adolf Hitler claimed he had the answer to these troubles, many listened.

The "Master Race"

Hitler declared that Germans of **Aryan** descent were part of the "Master Race" and that Jews, an inferior race, had conspired to ruin Germany. Thanks in part to a long tradition of **anti-Semitism,** many Germans began to believe his claims. More and more people joined Hitler's Nazi Party.

THE HOLOCAUST

Viewing the Holocaust Today

Philip Brooks

Heinemann Library
Chicago, Illinois

Designed by Joanna Sapwell
Photo research by Scott Braut
Originated by Ambassador Litho Ltd.
Printed in China, by Wing King Tong

07 06 05 04 03
10 9 8 7 6 5 4 3 2 1

**Library of Congress Cataloging-in-Publication
Data**
Brooks, Philip.
  Viewing the Holocaust today / Philip Brooks.
    p. cm. -- (The Holocaust)
Includes index.
Summary: Examines the movies, music, writings, and
museums that represent the victims and survivors of the
Holocaust.
  ISBN 1-4034-0815-7 (HC); 1-4034-3207-4 (Pbk.)
  1. Holocaust, Jewish (1939-1945)--Influence--Juvenile
literature. 2. Holocaust, Jewish (1939-1945), in literature--
Juvenile literature. 3. Holocaust, Jewish (1939-1945), in
motion pictures--Juvenile literature.
4. Holocaust memorials--Juvenile literature. [1. Holocaust,
Jewish (1939-1945), in motion pictures. 2. Holocaust,
Jewish (1939-1945), in literature. 3. Holocaust memorials.
4. Holocaust, Jewish (1939-1945)--Influence.] I. Title. II.
Holocaust (Chicago, Ill.)
  D804.34 .B76 2002
  940.53'18--dc21
                                      2002006854

Acknowledgments
The author and publisher are grateful to the following
for permission to reproduce copyright material:
p. 4 Bettmann/Corbis; pp. 5, 7, 23 Hulton Archive/Getty
Images; p. 6 Zydowski Instytut Historyczny Instytut
Nawwkowo-Badawczy/USHMM Photo Archives; pp. 8, 35
AFP/Corbis; p. 10 courtesy Ruth Meyerowitz; p. 11 Reuters
NewMedia, Inc./Corbis; p. 12 Michael St. Maur
Sheil/Corbis; p. 14 Alexander Kandolt, Staatliche Kusthalle
Karlsruhe; p. 15 courtesy Hector Feliciano; p. 16 Evy
Mages/New York Daily News/NewsCom; pp. 17, 19 The
Everett Collection; p. 18 AP Wide World Photo; p. 20 The
Kobal Collection/Picture Desk; p. 22 From Maus I: A
Survivor's Tale/My Father Bleeds History by Art
Spiegelman, copyright © 1973, 1980, 1981, 1982, 1984,
1985, 1986 by Art Spiegelman. Used by permission of
Pantheon Books, a division of Random House, Inc.; p. 24
Owen Franken/Corbis; p. 25 Ralf-Finn Hestoft/Corbis
SABA; p. 26 James P. Blair/Corbis; p. 27 Edward
Owen/USHMM Photo Archives; p. 28 Nik Wheeler/Corbis;
p. 30 USHMM Photo Archives; pp. 31, 32 Garo
Nalbandian/Israelimages.com; p. 33 courtesy Eisenmann
Architects; p. 34 Max Reid/USHMM Photo Archives; p. 37
Roberto Pfeil/AP Wide World Photo; p. 38 East
News/NewsCom; p. 39L Jonathan Evans/Reuters Photo
Archive/NewsCom; p. 39R Photonews/Topham/The Image
Works; p. 40 David Turnley/Corbis; p. 41 Sharon
Abady/AP Wide World Photos; p. 42 Piotr Malecki/Getty
Images/NewsCom; pp. 44, 45, 46, 47, 48, 49 Courtesy the
Liwazer Family

Cover photograph: (left) The Kobal Collection/Picture
Desk, (right) courtesy the Liwazer Family

Special thanks to Ronald Smelser and Sally Brown-Winter.

About the series consultants
Ronald Smelser is a history professor at the University
of Utah. He has written or edited eight books on Nazi
Germany and the Holocaust and over three dozen articles.
His recent publications include *Learning About the
Holocaust: A Student Guide* (4 vol.) and *Lessons and Legacies:
The Holocaust and Justice*. Professor Smelser is also a past
president of the German Studies Association.

Sally Brown-Winter has worked in the field of Jewish
Education as a principal and teacher for over 25 years.
In her schools, the Shoah—its history, lessons, and
implications—have been explored from kindergarten
through high school.

Every effort has been made to contact copyright holders of
any material reproduced in this book. Any omissions will
be rectified in subsequent printings if notice is given to
the publisher.

Some words are shown in bold, **like this.** You can find out what they mean
by looking in the glossary.

Contents

Introduction

What Was the Holocaust?

The Holocaust is the name given to the systematic persecution and murder of approximately six million Jewish people in Europe between 1939 and 1945. Germany's **Nazi** government carried out these crimes, sometimes with the aid, voluntary or involuntary, of government officials and citizens in other European countries.

The Holocaust began in Germany at the start of World War II. As Germany's armies swept across Poland, France, Holland, and beyond, they brought the destruction of Jewish communities. By 1945, six million of Europe's estimated nine million Jews were dead.

The Nazis also targeted other groups for mistreatment. Approximately 200,000 mentally and physically disabled people were killed. **Gypsies,** Poles, Russians, political enemies of the Nazi regime, homosexuals, and **Jehovah's Witnesses** were among the groups persecuted and in many cases murdered along with European Jews. During the war, German forces were also responsible for the deaths of three million Soviet **prisoners of war,** killed by starvation, exposure, beatings, and shootings.

Why Did it Happen?

Following its 1918 defeat in World War I, Germany experienced economic troubles. The Treaty of Paris that ended the war left Germany bankrupt and isolated. Ordinary Germans were going hungry and those who were better off grew tired of worrying about their country's future. So, when a strong-voiced, self-confident politician named Adolf Hitler claimed he had the answer to these troubles, many listened.

The "Master Race"

Hitler declared that Germans of **Aryan** descent were part of the "Master Race" and that Jews, an inferior race, had conspired to ruin Germany. Thanks in part to a long tradition of **anti-Semitism,** many Germans began to believe his claims. More and more people joined Hitler's Nazi Party.

Hitler's Power Grows

Hitler and his Nazis soon gathered enough followers to take over control of Germany. Between 1933 and 1936, he rose to become an all-powerful **dictator.** He commanded powerful armies that would soon sweep across Europe. A brutal secret police force called the **Gestapo,** and a highly-trained security unit called the *Schutzstaffel,* or **SS,** would soon carry out his orders to arrest, and later to destroy Germany's Jews.

Hitler explained that Germany's suffering could be blamed on its Jewish citizens.

The Troubles Begin

By 1933, life had gotten difficult for German Jews. Young Jewish men were beaten by groups of "Aryan men" wearing the brown-shirted uniforms of Hitler's Nazis. **Synagogues** and Jewish graveyards were vandalized. Nazis scrawled hateful graffiti on the windows of Jewish-owned businesses.

Jewish Denial

Many Jews fled Germany in the early 1930s. But despite Hitler's popularity and hateful policies, many others would not leave. They had fought for Germany in World War I and had lived in Germany all their lives. They refused to believe their country could turn on them. Other Jews wanted to leave, but did not have the money required to do so.

The Ghettos Are Established

Many Jewish businesses were looted and destroyed. Others were taken away from Jewish owners and given to members of the Nazi party. Later, Hitler decreed that Jews in most German cities had to leave their homes and live together behind walls in **ghettos.** As German armies took over in Poland and most of Europe, ghettos were established there, too. Nazis forced **rabbis** to cut off their long beards and made Jewish women clean public toilets with their bare hands.

The Final Solution

Soon, the Nazis decided that Jews were "life unworthy of life." By 1940, Hitler and his advisors undertook what they called the **Final Solution.** Now Jews who already endured crowded, unhealthy, and restrictive conditions in ghettos were rounded up and packed like cattle onto trains bound for specially-designed **concentration camps.** Some of these camps were designed as forced **labor camps,** others were **death camps.**

At labor camps, Jews and other **"undesirables"** were often killed through overwork, malnutrition, exposure, beatings, and bullets. At death camps like Auschwitz and Treblinka, the Nazis built specially-designed **gas chambers** for

murdering human beings as quickly and efficiently as possible, and ovens in which to burn the bodies. In the **gas chambers** of Auschwitz-Birkenau camp alone, 1.5 million people met their deaths between 1942 and 1945.

Why Did Citizens Let it Happen?

Many brave citizens of Germany and other countries hid Jews in their homes and worked to foil the **Nazis** during World War II. If caught, these people—part of what has come to be called the resistance—were arrested and sent to **concentration camps** or simply shot on the spot by the **Gestapo.** The kindness, decency, and strength of these people must never be forgotten.

Most people, however, did little to stop the Nazis. Many were simply too frightened to act. But Hitler's strong leadership led others to willingly accept the persecution of their neighbors. A vast number of German civilians claim they never knew

Jews were being killed. Countless witnesses claim that it required an act of will not to know.

In the towns and villages of Poland and other countries with histories of **anti-Semitism,** local citizens often proved willing to help the Germans find and arrest their Jewish neighbors. After the Holocaust and World War II ended, some Jewish survivors who returned to their villages to reclaim homes and farms were chased away or even murdered.

The Killing Spreads

In 1939, German armies attacked Poland. World War II had begun. In June of 1941, after invading the Soviet Union, Nazi forces included **SS** and police assigned to **Einsatzgruppen.** They carried out mass-

Poniatowa Labor Camp

Poniatowa **labor camp** was built in a forest in Poland in 1941. Prisoners either worked in sewing workshops or on road construction in the surrounding forest. Here, a guard beats a prisoner at the camp.

Dwight Eisenhower, a U.S. general put in charge of dealing with the camps, made sure that extensive photographs were taken and movies were filmed. He worried that U.S. citizens at home might not believe what Germany had done. This picture was taken on May 3, 1945. Young prisoners cheer the U.S. troops who liberated the camp.

murder operations against Jews, **gypsies,** and **Communist** government officials.

Between 1941 and 1944, much of Europe fell under Hitler's shadow. Several million innocent people were forced onto trucks and trains and taken away to concentration camps. Under Hitler's rule, new laws forced Jews to wear yellow stars that identified them as inferior and specifically Jewish— other "inferior" groups wore different colored stars.

Allied Victory and Liberation

Only Germany's surrender to U.S. and Soviet forces in 1945 stopped the slaughter. In many cases, retreating German forces tried to destroy evidence. They dynamited buildings and burned records as they fled. But there was simply too much to hide. When soldiers from the United States, Great Britain, and the Soviet Union entered the concentration camps, what they found

made many weep or become sick. Stiff corpses piled like wood, blankly staring survivors like living skeletons, ovens built to dispose of murdered people: visions to haunt these soldiers and humanity forever.

Hitler and many of his top officials committed suicide in 1945. Others faced war crimes trials and were hung or imprisoned. Still others escaped detection or were only arrested years later.

The thousands who survived the camps long enough to be **liberated** spent time in special **displaced persons camps** where they were nursed back to health. Most searched for missing family members or spouses to no avail. Others were reunited. Unable to return to their homes, many became people without countries or families. They scattered throughout the world. Many survivors **emigrated** to Israel and the United States to rebuild their lives.

The Survivors Today

Children and Grandchildren of Survivors

Writer and child of Holocaust survivors Thane Rosenbaum has said, "the enormity of Auschwitz was so great that it can't be canceled out in one generation. It lives, it breeds, it carries on. It has its own life and it's living it through children [of survivors]."

Seventy-five thousand Holocaust survivors eventually settled in the United States. Together they had 250,000 children. This second generation often call themselves "2G'ers." Many come together in person or use the Internet to share their feelings. Children of survivors often worrying about burdening their parents with "unimportant" problems.

Feeling Different

All families are different, each has its own way of dealing with troubles. Some parents who survived the Holocaust have shared these experiences with their children, others never speak of the past.

Many children of survivors were born in **displaced person camps** to mothers and fathers who had often lost their entire extended family and all of their possessions. Survivors tend to be extremely protective of their children, wanting to shield them from all of life's difficulties to make up for the horrors they suffered during their own childhood.

The Third Generation

On a website dedicated to "3G'ers"—the grandchildren of survivors—Gilad Evrony wrote extensively about his grandfather. His words give some perspective on the gratitude and guilt felt by the generations who followed the survivors:

My grandfather's story always causes me to look at myself and think. It makes me think about the value of life, the struggle for survival, and the precious things for which

A-15803

Lello Perugia received this tattoo while he was an inmate at Auschwitz. He was sent to the camp from Italy with his four brothers. Three did not survive.

one must always be thankful. Whenever I see the wonderful family that my grandfather helped create, I wonder what would have happened had he not survived... My grandfather's survival story has always given me belief that life always prevails. I grew up with my mother talking about the Holocaust; it became an innate part of me. I grew up hearing stories and people related to me that we're always shrouded in this thing called the Holocaust. It was not until much later that I realized the whole story. Innocently enough, I used to tease with my grandfather that every time I recited the engraved number on his arm by heart, I would get a dollar. Being only eight years old at the time, it seemed like only a game...

Of all the emotions conjured up by my grandfather's story, one stands out the most. Here I am sitting in a beautiful house, free from oppression, free from hunger, free from anything which could restrict my freedom, yet only fifty years ago, six million Jews experienced exactly the opposite. They went through a hell which I cannot even fathom. I was filled with feelings of guilt, horror, and sadness, yet at the same time I was incredibly happy. I marveled at the miraculous change that my grandfather and the Jews as a whole underwent. Israel has been established, a dream which has gone unfulfilled for 2,000 years. The Holocaust survivors have regenerated the Jewish nation by creating successful families and new communities...

Such mixed feelings—of admiration and gratitude for the men and women who managed to live long enough to be **liberated,** sadness for those who died, and guilt over being lucky enough to live in the United States—are typical of the generations who followed the survivors.

Witnesses

Despite all the evil work done in the camps and later during the death marches of 1945, tens of thousands of Jews and others were liberated by **Allied Forces.** Almost all spoke of the need to bear witness on behalf of those who were not so lucky.

Testimony

In 1994, filmmaker Steven Spielberg established the Survivors of the Shoah Visual History Foundation. The organization has videotaped the testimony of more than 51,000 survivors and witnesses of the Holocaust. Spielberg has said that each person who testifies becomes "a teacher, putting a real face, a real voice, a real experience in front of this and future generations."

Challenges of Gathering Testimony

The Shoah Foundation has gathered interviews in 57 different countries. Interviewing people outside of North America sometimes poses special challenges. In the United States, people are more likely to tell strangers about their private lives than in many other places. Also, many people who lived in

countries without freedom of speech and religion were frightened to reveal their stories. Jewish survivors living in the former Soviet Union, for instance, often experienced **anti-Semitism** and discrimination long after the Holocaust and did not want to call attention to themselves.

In some cases, the interviews were collected in the same towns and villages where **Nazi** atrocities took place. Remarkably, victims, witnesses, members of the resistance, and collaborators often still lived side by side. This made some survivors and witnesses hesitant to tell their stories.

A Painful Legacy for Germans, Too

The history of the Holocaust presents difficulties for non-Jews, too. Bill Bradley, a past presidential candidate and former Senator from New Jersey, is married to Ernestine Bradley. Ernestine grew up in a German town named Passau. She was the daughter of a **_Luftwaffe_** pilot in World War II. As an adult living in the United States, she had often asked her parents what they knew about what happened to the Jews in the 1940s. She pressed her mother for details. Had there been Jews living in Passau? "Oh, yeah," her mother replied, "there were Jews, and they had department stores."

"Where did they go?" Ernestine demanded.

"I don't know, but they left," her mother told her.

No "Normal Life"

No survivor has completely left the camps behind them. Survivor Ruth Meyerowitz explained this in an interview given 60 years after her time spent in Auschwitz. Every day, something reminds her of the camps:

*The **crematorium** was just a… few minutes away. We could see the chimneys from… wherever we were and of course we could smell the gas when it was… let out from the **gas chambers**… And then we could smell the burning of the bodies, the human flesh burning. And then they cleared the grates and we could hear the grates being cleaned, and it's similar to what your own oven would be like when you move the grates around except… it was much noisier so that we could hear it all the way in the barracks. And, to this day when I clean my own oven, I am reminded of that noise of the cleaning of the grates in the crematorium.*

The answer upset and angered Bradley. How, she wondered, could you let your neighbors disappear without trying to find out what had happened to them?

When Bradley challenged her father as to what he knew about the plight of the Jews, he told her a story about giving his ration card to a Jewish couple forced to wear the yellow Star of David on their coats.

"He thought that story was very nice," Bradley recalled in an interview. "And I said, 'So you knew they didn't get enough food.'" Her father admitted he knew Jews were hungry. But he insisted he knew nothing of the **concentration camps.**

Until his death, her father denied any knowledge that Jews and others were being murdered. "I think there were ways of not wanting to know," she says sadly. Even though she was a child at the time, Bradley's connection to the Holocaust fills her with grief and even guilt. "It has taken me years," she says, "to face it directly."

The Need to Know

In the chaos that followed World War II, it was often impossible for **liberated** survivors to know what had happened to their families. Had parents, grandparents, children, uncles, aunts, cousins, friends, and neighbors made it out alive? Had they avoided the camps by hiding? Or fought as members of the resistance and lived in the woods? Had any managed to obtain false papers that allowed them to **emigrate** somewhere safe? The Germans kept detailed records about who entered the camps, though some of these records were destroyed by the Nazis at the end of the

A Difficult Past

Ernestine Bradley takes comfort in deep friendships she's formed with a number of Holocaust survivors during her struggle to deal with her family's past.

11

war. Still, it would take years to untangle the stories of families and many remain unsure today as to exactly what happened to loved ones when they fell into the hands of the **Nazis.**

A New Way to Search

The Internet has become a powerful tool to search for separated family members. Reading some of the messages posted on electronic bulletin boards reveals the pain of not knowing. A successful young doctor, writes:

> *To whom it may concern: I am the grandson of Manfred Kropf who died in Auschwitz in 1944. My birth parents gave me up for adoption at age 1-2 in Germany due to their impoverished state. I am trying to find them to be reunited with them....*

Others express hope that reports of a death were inaccurate. A thirteen-year-old girl named Miriam has posted a note on another board dedicated to reuniting families. She writes:

> *I am 13 and am namesake to a girl who "died" in the Holocaust. I put that in quotes because while I was visiting the Old Jewish Town in Prague, we found a picture gallery that had drawings by children in Terezín [**ghetto**]. Under the picture that I recognized as my namesake's it said that she survived the Holocaust! I was awed by this and made it my goal to find her and meet her someday! If there is anybody who could point my toes in the right direction, I'd be grateful...*

Reparations: Trying to Fix the Unfixable

Recently, efforts have been made to recover some of the valuables and money stolen from Jews by the Nazi government. When the Nazis arrested Jews, they stole their life insurance policies—often worth large sums. They looted bank accounts and stole art collections, too.

"Wall of Death"

The "Wall of Death" is located between Barrack 10 and 11 at Auschwitz. Thousands of prisoners were executed by shooting at the wall. Today, schoolchildren often visit the wall to commemorate the people who died at the spot.

Some wealthy Holocaust victims hid their assets in secret Swiss bank accounts before being deported to **concentration camps.** Swiss banking laws call for the identity of account holders to remain secret. These laws protected assets. However, these same laws also meant that accounts belonging to Jews killed by the **Final Solution** could not be handed over to the families to whom they belonged. Fifty or sixty years later, Swiss banks were still reluctant to provide information concerning account holders.

Today, heirs to this stolen property can submit claims through the United States government to have some or all of it returned. In addition, the German government has passed a series of laws that allow heirs and survivors to claim wages for the slave labor they were forced to perform.

IF Farben, a huge chemical company, and Krupp, at the time a **munitions** manufacturer, used imprisoned Jews as laborers in their factories and labs. Today, those former prisoners and their families may submit documentation to receive payment for that work. Clearly, it is not so much the money as the principle that drives families to pursue these claims. The money represents an apology or at least acknowledgment on the part of corporations involved that they benefited from Nazi crimes.

IBM and the Holocaust

International Business Machines, a U.S. corporation better known as IBM, also profited as a result of the Holocaust. IBM's punch-card machines—early versions of computers—were sold to the Nazi government to help them count Germany's population in 1933 and 1939. The machine allowed Hitler's government to create lists of Jewish citizens and where they lived quickly and efficiently.

Author Edwin Black claims in his book, *IBM and the Holocaust,* that IBM executives continued to sell the Nazis new and improved machines even after learning this technology aided in the commission of crimes against Jews, **gypsies,** and others. IBM acknowledges that its machinery was used by the Nazis, but denies Black's claims that they profited knowingly from human suffering. IBM has since contributed money to a reparations fund in Germany.

Stolen Art

During the Holocaust, thousands of paintings and sculptures were either stolen by the Nazis or left behind in the homes of Jews who had fled or been arrested. The stolen art has often been sold and resold, donated to museums, or passed from one family member to another with no knowledge of its origin. In the past, a few museums had attempted to block efforts to return stolen art, fearing their collections would be diminished.

A Painting Returned

In 2001, an important painting, *Olevano* by Alexander Kanoldt, that had belonged to a man named Dr. Ismar Littman was returned to his family. Littman was a prominent Jewish attorney in Poland. He loved fine art and was a well-known collector. By 1934, Jews in Poland faced persecution, humiliation, and worse. Unable to stand the strain, Dr. Littman committed suicide. Some of his large art collection was hurriedly sold by his family at bargain prices before it could be looted by Polish authorities. The rest fell into the hands of these corrupt officials.

Olevano, one of Dr. Littman's most beloved and valuable paintings, was returned to his heirs through the work of the Holocaust Claims Processing Office in New York. The painting was put on display at New York's Museum of Jewish Heritage to celebrate its return. At the painting's unveiling, Dr. Willi Korte, speaking on behalf of Dr. Littman's heirs said, "[We] have received today an important work of art that [we] have long sought...We are particularly pleased that the National Gallery in Berlin recognized that the 1935 forced sale was unlawful and unjust... It gives us great pleasure to make the painting, together with its entire tragic history, available to the public."

The Lost Museum

A man named Hector Feliciano has dedicated a good deal of his life to retrieving looted art. Feliciano was born in Puerto Rico. He attended college in the United States, became a journalist, and moved to Paris. In Paris, he became aware of the fact that a good deal of art that ended up in French museums after World War II had been stolen from Jewish collectors. He was shocked to find that museums were glad to have the works and were unwilling to search for the rightful owners.

Through three years of research and with the help of gallery insiders willing to reveal where paintings and sculptures came from, Feliciano broke the silence with his 1997 book, *The Lost Museum: The Nazi Conspiracy to Steal the World's Greatest Works of Art*. Until Feliciano's work, Holocaust survivors had done little to get justice. "They said they were so happy to live that they didn't ask for material things," Feliciano explains. He adds the sad truth that those left alive also felt guilty asking for what rightly belonged to them. "They were guilty to have survived," he says.

The book brought public pressure on French art galleries to display 2,000 works of art that had previously been hidden in national collections. Following the exhibit, dozens of claims were filed by families around the world who previously believed their art had been lost or destroyed during the war. These claims must be confirmed and legal work can take years to complete, but many works of art are slowly finding their way to the rightful owners.

Germany and Israel

Israel was established in 1948. The German Democratic Republic, also known as West Germany, did much to help the State of Israel as the new country struggled to survive.

Following the Holocaust, many in the newly-created state of Israel wanted no help from the Germans. Many survivors and protesters were upset by the idea that Germany might be allowed to atone for its sins by paying money. But in 1952, a deeply divided Israeli government decided to accept reparations.

West Germany—and today a united Germany—has provided about $60 billion in cash and manufactured goods to Israel and Holocaust survivors. Contemporary Germany is a strong democracy and an ally of the United States and supports the existence of Israel.

Hector Feliciano

In addition to the United States, *The Lost Museum* has been published in France, Germany, Japan, and Korea. Feliciano now gives lectures based on the book.

The Holocaust in Today's Movies, Writings, and Music

Abraham Foxman, the national director of the Anti-Defamation League and a Holocaust survivor wrote:

> Today there is far too much trivialization of Holocaust imagery. A rude shop keeper is called the Soup **Nazi,** someone who cuts off another driver is called a traffic Nazi... A party in a business dispute is called a Hitler. Legal adversaries accuse each other of **Gestapo** tactics. Fashion designers create "Nazi" collections; a rap group called **Concentration Camp** II releases an album titled Da Halocaust.

His argument is important. Words have power and must be used carefully. Hitler was a mass murderer, not just a mean and unreasonable man. The Gestapo burst into peoples homes in the middle of the night and dragged them off to be killed in concentration camps. Nazi uniforms are symbols of hatred and destruction to Jews and others around the world.

A Difficult Subject

The Holocaust is a very difficult subject to portray. Even well-meaning attempts may offend and insult those who suffered. For instance, the publishers of Superman comic books devoted three issues to sending the superhero back in time to fight the Nazis. But the Nazis' victims were never referred to as "Jews." The writers had meant to create the idea that the Nazis were evil and that everyone was a victim. Instead, Holocaust victims felt that they were being left out of the story. The Nazis killed Jews for the simple reason they were Jews. Children reading the comic books, survivors argued, should know that.

Shoah

Shoah, the title of Claude Lanzmann's 1985 documentary, means "chaos" or "total destruction" in Hebrew. Shoah is the name Israelis have given to the Holocaust.

The "Soup Nazi"

The "Soup Nazi" character on the popular TV show *Seinfeld* was based on Chef Al Yefganeh, shown here at his restaurant, the International Soup Kitchen. On the show, the Soup Nazi was portrayed as a very rude man who refused to serve soup to certain people.

The Train to Treblinka

Claude Lanzmann interviewed Henrik Gowkowski for his film, *Shoah*. Henrik was a train engineer who transported Jews to the **death camp** of Treblinka in Poland.

To make *Shoah*, Lanzmann spent six years looking for witnesses to the Holocaust. He interviewed hundreds of Germans and Poles who either worked in the camps or saw what went on in them. While witnesses are interviewed, we see current pictures of the places they describe. We see that grass and flowers now grow on the mass graves. New trains use the same railroad tracks that brought victims to the concentration camps. The camps themselves look like abandoned factories.

At one point, Lanzmann calmly interviews a railway engineer who used to drive trains to Treblinka, a concentration camp in Poland. He asks the man if he could hear what went on in the boxcars behind his locomotive.

"The screams from the cars closest to the locomotives could be heard," the man says.

"Can one get used to that?" asks Lanzmann.

"No," says the engineer. He goes on to explain how the Germans kept him and other workers drunk so that they could stand to do the job.

In another interview we meet Filip Muller, a Czech Jew who was assigned by German guards to stand at Auschwitz's **crematorium** doors as victims were marched inside. Muller tells Lanzmann that one day a group of Czech's were being sent to their deaths. They were singing *Hatikvah* (a Jewish prayer) and then the Czech national anthem. Filled with terrible grief, Muller decided to join them in the **gas chamber.** But as he entered, a woman stopped him: "Your death won't give us back our lives," she begged him. "That's no way. You must get out of here alive, you must bear witness to our suffering and to the injustice done to us."

Lanzmann's nine-hour film brings the past into the present as we watch people describe what they saw so many years before.

Schindler's List

When Steven Spielberg set out to make *Schindler's List*, he worried he could not do justice to such an important subject matter. The director of *Jaws*, *E.T.*, and *Jurassic Park* wanted to make the film for ten years, but various factors delayed the project.

The movie's main character is German businessman Oskar Schindler. It is Poland in the 1940s, so the best way to do well in business is to befriend **Nazi** officers. Early in the film, Schindler, a non-Jew, spends time and money befriending the Nazis and seems uninterested in the crimes they may be committing. These friends soon allow him to take over a factory stolen from its Jewish owner. Schindler is then provided with Jewish prisoners from a nearby **labor camp.** Schindler makes one of the inmates, Itzhak Stern, his accountant. Under Stern's influence, Schindler comes to feel responsible for his workers. When it is decided that the Jews working at Schindler's factory will be confined to a camp run by the sadistic killer Amon Goeth, Schindler volunteers to keep "his Jews" at the factory instead. He pays for construction of barracks and barbed wire fences. Schindler convinces Goeth and others that his factory is just another part of the labor camp when, in fact, it becomes a safe haven.

Schindler continues to run a profitable business, but grows more and more involved with the plight of his Jewish workers. At one point, a young Jewish woman comes to Schindler and begs him to hire her parents. They are at Goeth's camp and she is very worried they will be sent to the ovens at Auschwitz. He becomes enraged with her—he says that he will not hire them, that he is running a business, not a safe haven for Jews.

Amon Goeth

Actor Ralph Fiennes portrayed Amon Goeth in *Schindler's List*. In this scene, he selects a prisoner for his housemaid.

Oskar and Itzhak

Actor Ben Kingsley, who played accountant Itzhak Stern, believes *Schindler's List* was important to make because "this period of history must be retold to every generation… We have a long, long way to go before stories like this become ancient history."

A week later, he trades his watch for her parents and brings them to his factory.

By the end of the film, Schindler and Stern agonize over the creation of a list of names—workers Schindler will be allowed to keep, while the others will be killed. He is devastated by the fact he cannot save everyone.

Schindler's List was originally a book by Thomas Keneally. Many of the episodes written by Keneally were true. A scene in which a young man named Poldek Pfefferberg escapes a roundup of Jews by convincing a German commander that he had been ordered to collect and pile up suitcases really happened. Oskar

Schindler really did win the life of a Nazi commander's Jewish maid in a hand of blackjack.

The film raised Spielberg's own awareness about his connection to the Holocaust. The outpouring of gratitude paid to him by survivors who felt he had honored them with his work inspired him to found the Shoah Foundation. "No one can do anything to fix the past—that's already happened," said Spielberg. "But a picture like this can impact on us, delivering a mandate about what must never happen again." The movie won Academy Awards for Best Picture and Best Director in 1992.

Life is Beautiful

Roberto Benigni has said about his movie, *Life is Beautiful*, "I wanted to make a beautiful movie, and especially to say something poetic." Not everyone felt he was successful. During a press conference at the Cannes Film Festival in France, one journalist stood up and accused Benigni

of making fun of Holocaust victims. A reporter from the International Herald Tribune agreed. "I loathed this film," she said. The movie reviewer for the London Guardian newspaper called the movie "a hopelessly inadequate memorial to the vile events of the Holocaust."

Other critics and moviegoers believed the film was a work of genius. Many saw the film as a fable about the Holocaust, not an attempt to portray the day-to-day reality of life in a **concentration camp** but a comment upon human nature. The State of Israel invited Benigni, an Italian, to screen the film at the Jerusalem Film Festival. Jerusalem's mayor awarded the actor/director with a special commendation. The mayor thanked Benigni for "furthering the universal understanding of Jewish history."

In the movie, Guido, played by Benigni, turns life in a concentration camp into an elaborate game in order to save his son from knowing the truth. The movie is not meant to be realistic, yet realistic elements are introduced. The concentration camp, for instance, has some of the same architecture as Auschwitz. We see train

tracks running into the infamous arched gateway. Yet, this camp is clean and there is little cruelty or death actually shown on screen.

The movie is often very funny and touching. Upon arrival, Guido tells his son that they are now involved in a game. The goal, he convinces his child, is to be the first to amass 1,000 points. Guido's jokes and horsing around become acts of resistance meant to distract his son from the truth: they are doomed.

"Whether people feel that this is a film that should or should not have been made," Benigni has said, "at that moment of

A Movie by a Comedian

The film *Life is Beautiful* contains some very funny moments. But Roberto Benigni insists he did not make a comedy about the Holocaust. The movie is, he says, a movie by a comedian about the Holocaust.

my life, this was the only thing I could make. And if I could come back, I would remake this movie. It's the thing that I love most in my life. It's the best thing I can produce."

The Producers

The Producers is a Mel Brooks' musical comedy about staging the worst Broadway musical show ever. The main characters, a theatrical producer named Max Bialystock and an accountant named Leo Bloom, figure they can get rich if they raise money from investors to put on a play that will be so bad it closes down after only one performance. Their idea for the worst musical ever, a show that is in such bad taste it will be booed off the stage? A musical version of the life of Adolf Hitler.

The Hitler musical is—to the horror of Bialystock and Bloom—a smash hit, despite such musical dance numbers as "Springtime for Hitler" with lyrics like "Don't be stupid! Be a smarty! Come and join the **Nazi** Party!"

The Producers was originally a 1968 Mel Brooks movie. At the time, some thought the movie was hilarious. Others thought it was in bad taste. Brooks won an Academy Award for Best Screenplay. As the events of the Holocaust move farther behind us, perhaps we are able to laugh a little more easily at jokes about the Nazis. Also, *The Producers* makes its jokes always at the expense of Hitler and the Nazis and never their victims.

Judging from the many Tony Award nominations and awards the show received, and the fact that tickets are nearly impossible to get, most theatergoers seem to find the show to be much more funny than offensive.

Showing the Unthinkable

If you wish to make a movie about life in the camps, how much should you show? The reality of what happened is often too terrible to put on screen, but if you soften the horror to make the movie easier to watch, you may have told a lie about history.

Filmmakers can never put on screen the absolute truth of how terrible it was to die in Auschwitz. Remember, this was a place where people were herded into **gas chambers** and murdered with **cyanide.** Dead bodies were thrown into ovens by other enslaved inmates who themselves were later murdered and disposed of in the same way.

If you leave out some of the worst details of the Holocaust, have you not somehow wronged the memory of those people who suffered and died?

Writing About the Holocaust

Believe it or not, two of the better books about the Holocaust are comic books. *Maus I: My Father Bleeds History* and *Maus II: And Here My Troubles Began,* written and drawn by Art Spiegelman, portray Jews as mice, Nazis as cats, Polish people

as pigs, and Americans as dogs. *Maus* won a Pulitzer Prize in 1992. The books are often taught in schools.

The first book traces Spiegelman's father's real experiences during the Holocaust and also the making of the comic book itself. Day after day Art, drawn as a mouse, talks, listens, and fights with his aging father.

Maus

Maus accomplishes two things: it relates the conditions of Polish concentration camps, while also depicting the difficult time children of survivors have coming to terms with the horrendous plight of their ancestors. *Maus* is not only a narrative of the Holocaust, but also a story of human struggle and suffering—not just of one generation, but also of succeeding ones.

The two end up exploring the pain they have shared and never discussed, including the suicide of Anja, wife and mother. As the story shifts back and forth from 1940s Europe to the contemporary United States, we see some of the difficulties faced by survivors and children of survivors.

Maus I recounts Vladek Spiegelman's experiences up until his time in Auschwitz **concentration camp.** *Maus II* tells of his terrible days in "Mauschwitz," his **liberation** and reunion with his wife, Anja, and his life afterwards. Even in comic book form, the details of the horrors found in the camps is upsetting.

The Most Widely Read Diary in the World

The most famous book to come out of the Holocaust was written by a thirteen-year-old girl. The world is lucky that Anne Frank kept a diary while she and her family hid from the **Nazis** in an Amsterdam attic from 1942 to 1944. Her entries reveal an intelligent and lively writer engaged in her immediate surroundings, while at the same time aware that Nazi terror was moving closer and closer.

Anne Frank died of **typhus** in Bergen-Belsen concentration camp in 1945. Her father, Otto, survived and the diary was returned to him by Miep Gies, one of the people who helped hide the Frank family. Convinced it was an important document, he had it published. But he removed passages that he felt would be hurtful to people still alive and others passages he found upsetting.

In 1995, amid controversy as to whether the book "belonged" to Otto or to the world, the diary was republished in its complete form. One can picture Anne Frank hiding in the crowded attic, always afraid that on that night the **Gestapo** will take her family away, as she writes:

I simply can't build up my hopes on a foundation consisting of confusion, misery and death. I see the world gradually being turned into a wilderness; I hear the ever approaching thunder, which will destroy us too; I can feel the sufferings of millions; and yet, if I look up into the heavens, I think that it will all come out right, that this cruelty will end, and that peace and tranquillity will return again... I must uphold my ideals, for perhaps the time will come when I shall be able to carry them out.

Elie Wiesel's Testimony

Night, Elie Wiesel's autobiographical novel, traces his boyhood experiences in the Hungarian village of Sighet (now Romania) and then Auschwitz and

Anne's Diary

These pages are part of Anne Frank's diary from October 1942. The most famous passage of the diary, the one most often quoted states: "I still believe, in spite of everything, that people are still truly good at heart."

Buchenwald **concentration camps.** As a boy growing up in a religious home, Wiesel spent his days studying the Talmud, an ancient Jewish text. When the **Nazis** took over Hungary and Romania, he and his family were forced into a **ghetto** and then were deported along with about 13,000 other Jews to Auschwitz. Wiesel was not yet sixteen years old.

Upon arrival at Birkenau, the receiving area at the Auschwitz camp, Elie and his father were separated from his mother and younger sister who were immediately killed in the **gas chambers.** Of this experience Wiesel writes in *Night*:

> *Never shall I forget that night, the first night in camp, which has turned my life into one long night, seven times cursed and seven times sealed…. Never shall I forget those moments which murdered my God and my soul and turned my dreams to dust. Never shall I forget these things, even if I am condemned to live as long as God Himself. Never.*

During the next year, Elie and his father survive cruelty, disease, overwork, and hunger in Auschwitz. Elie also struggles with the question of how God could allow such things to happen and such evil men to exist. Wiesel loses his faith. Following a death march to Buchenwald, a camp inside Germany, Wiesel loses his ailing father as well.

After his **liberation** from Buchenwald, Wiesel sees himself in a mirror for the first time in a year: "From the depths of the mirror, a corpse gazed back at me. The look in his eyes, as they stared into mine, has never left me."

In an essay called "Why I Write," Wiesel states: "I never intended to be a novelist. The only role I sought was that of witness. I believed that, having survived by chance, I was duty-bound to give meaning to my survival, to justify each moment of my life. I knew the story had to be told…"

Wiesel wrote *Night* in his native Yiddish in 1958. First released in English in 1960, the book shocked the world and renewed focus on the events of the Holocaust. To date, Wiesel has written more than

Writing Around the Holocaust

Most of Wiesel's novels take place either before or after the Holocaust. He states, "when I see that it becomes tolerable, I don't speak about it. That's why I have written so little about the Holocaust."

40 books. He received the Nobel Peace Prize in 1986, both for his contributions to literature and commitment to fighting injustice and hatred throughout the world.

Wagner in Israel

Composer Richard Wagner (1813–1883) was Hitler's favorite. His music was heard at Nazi rallies and in concentration camps. Wagner himself, besides being a great artist, was an outspoken **anti-Semite.** Although many of the conductors and musicians considered to be the best interpreters of Wagner's work have been Jews, his music was not performed in Israel until 1981.

In July 2001, Daniel Barenboim, an Argentine-born Jew who grew up in Israel, decided to conduct music from a Wagner opera at the Israel Festival to be held in Jerusalem. There were many protests. The music, it was argued, offended many of the 350,000 Holocaust survivors in the country. Others, including many survivors, supported Barenboim on the grounds of artistic freedom. In the end, he reluctantly agreed to replace the Wagner piece with one by Schumann. Then, at the end of the concert, he announced that the orchestra would play music by Wagner for those who wished to stay and listen.

When the piece began, there were some noisy protests from the audience and many banged the hall's doors as they left. "I don't want to hurt anybody and I don't want to force anybody to hear something they don't want to or cannot because of dreadful associations," he said. But Barenboim felt strongly that others should not be denied hearing Wagner's magnificent music.

Michael Avraham, a 67-year-old engineer, agreed with Barenboim's decision to let the work be heard and stayed to hear the music. "You don't have to listen," he told some young protesters. "You can go home. You didn't go through the Holocaust. I did."

The United States Holocaust Memorial Museum

At the end of World War II, a majority of Holocaust survivors **emigrated** to Israel and the United States. The Israeli government created a Holocaust Museum and Memorial in 1953. For many years, survivors and their families in the United States called for the creation of a place where American children could learn about what happened in Europe during the 1930s and 1940s.

How the Museum Came to Be

When Miles Lerman was a young man, he was arrested by the **Nazis** and sent to a **labor camp** near Lvov, Poland. Lerman soon escaped from the labor camp and fought with the Polish resistance— attacking Nazi fuel depots and patrols, and stealing food. When the war ended, he learned that his entire family had died in Belzec **concentration camp.**

After the war, Lerman moved to the United States, married another survivor, and ran a successful business in New Jersey. He and his wife believed it was their duty to testify about what had happened during WWII. They spoke to as many young people as possible about all they'd seen and experienced.

But they wanted to do more. Miles Lerman and many Americans felt strongly that the United States should create a memorial to the victims of the Holocaust and a museum to teach about what happens when hatred is allowed to flourish. President Jimmy Carter, and author and survivor Elie Wiesel joined Lerman in calling for such a place. After much work, it was decided that a U.S. Holocaust Memorial Museum would be built near the Washington Monument in Washington, D.C.

The Museum's Mission

Today, the United States Holocaust Memorial Museum includes in its mission statement the goal to become:

America's national institution for the documentation, study, and interpretation of Holocaust history, and [to] serve as this country's memorial to the millions of people murdered during the Holocaust…The Museum's primary mission is to advance and disseminate knowledge about this unprecedented tragedy; to preserve the memory of those who suffered; and to encourage its visitors to reflect upon the moral and spiritual questions raised by the events of the Holocaust as well as their own responsibilities as citizens of a democracy.

From Citizens to Outcasts

This is part of a permanent display at the U.S. Holocaust Memorial Museum, *From Citizens to Outcasts*, located on the fourth floor.

The new institution would commemorate and tell the story of all the Nazi's victims, Jews and non-Jews, and work to prevent such a thing from ever happening again. Lerman, Wiesel, and others worked to raise money to build the museum and to gain access to Nazi records and artifacts.

The Planning

Now that it was agreed that the museum would be built, and where it would stand, the most difficult question had to be answered. What should a building with such an important purpose look like? The task of answering such questions of design fell to a famous architect named James Ingo Freed. Freed, a Jew, had lived in Germany during much of his childhood. He and his sister were sent to the U.S. in 1939. His parents joined them in 1941.

Freed studied the Holocaust extensively, learning and seeing all he could before sitting down to imagine a suitable structure and get it on paper. He toured Auschwitz and other camps. A vision began to take shape in his mind. The barbed wire fences, ugly brick buildings, and imposing guard towers would be hinted at in his design.

The building he created is haunted by the references he made to the camps. There are spaces that feel claustrophobic, cold, and mournful. There are beautiful spaces as well, filled with light.

The United States Holocaust Memorial Museum is one of the most visited attractions in Washington, D.C. More than 17.2 million people have entered its doors since the day it opened, April 23, 1993.

Other Holocaust Museums

The Musee Memorial des Enfants d'Izieu

The Musee Memorial des Enfants d'Izieu (The Memorial Museum for the Children of Izieu) in France is notable for its focus on Jewish children caught in the Holocaust. When **Nazi** armies took over France in 1940, French Jews were in trouble. Only a few organizations worked to help Jews. The Oeuvre de Secours aux Enfants, a Jewish childrens' aid association, worked to gain the release of young people arrested and imprisoned by the Nazis. In 1941, a woman named Sabine Zlatin helped found a shelter for these children.

But soon, Nazi pressure reached them again and 44 children and the 7 adults who supervised them moved hurriedly to a large house overlooking the Rhone River, in the small village of Izieu. They were safe for a while. Then, in February 1944, the charity was forced to shut down all of its children's homes. In the beginning of April, Sabine Zlatin left Izieu for a few days to seek the help of a Catholic priest in a nearby city. While still away, news reached her that the **Gestapo** had come to Izieu.

On April 6, 1944, as the children were about to have breakfast, a car burst into the courtyard along with two trucks. Everyone present was arrested. Someone had informed the Nazis that Jews were being hidden there. Thirty-four children and four adults were sent to Auschwitz-Birkenau—all but one died there. In 1994, the French government commemorated these terrible events by making the house and barn where the children had been sheltered into a museum. Visitors can see the supervisors' room, the dormitories, and the dining hall. Some of the childrens' letters and drawings are also on display.

Museum Memorial Library

The Holocaust Museum Houston is an education center, as well as a memorial. The Boniuk Library and Resource Center in the museum has more than 4,000 books on the history of Jews, the Holocaust, post-Holocaust, and related subjects. Archives are also in the library—most of which have been donated by survivors and World War II veterans from around the country.

The Mechelen Museum of Deportation and Resistance

For centuries, Mechelen was an ordinary Belgian town lying between Brussels and Antwerp. When German soldiers took over the country, that changed. On July 25, 1942, Nazi officials ordered 10,000 Jews to report for "labor mobilization." Two days later, the Dossin barracks in Mechelen were seized for use as a holding area for Jews they planned to deport. Over the next two years, approximately 25,000 Belgian Jews were sent first to Mechelen and then to Auschwitz in Poland. Only about 1,200 survived.

Today, those barracks have been made into The Mechelen Museum of Deportation and Resistance. In the Shoah museum, the dead are commemorated. The museum also celebrates the fact that about half of Belgium's Jews survived the war, including 4,000 children. The survival rate was higher than in other parts of Europe thanks to many Belgian government officials who refused to cooperate with deportation orders, ordinary citizens who hid Jews, and resistance fighters who made the hunt for Jews more difficult and dangerous for German forces.

Holocaust Museum Houston

The permanent exhibit at the core of the Holocaust Museum Houston in Texas is called *Bearing Witness: A Community Remembers.* The Houston museum is unique in that it focuses on survivors living in the area. During 2001, the museum sponsored *Private Writings, Public Records: Diaries of Young People in the Holocaust.* The exhibition gathered diaries written by children during the Holocaust.

Other Museums and Memorials

Below are just a few of the other Holocaust Museums and Memorials in the United States:

- C.A.N.D.L.E.S. (Children of Auschwitz Nazi Deadly Lab Experiments Survivors) Museum, Terre Haute, IN
- Dallas Holocaust Memorial Center, Dallas, TX
- Desert Holocaust Memorial, Rancho Mirage, CA
- Detroit Holocaust Memorial Center, West Bloomfield, MI
- El Paso Holocaust Museum and Study Center, El Paso, TX
- Florida Holocaust Museum, St. Petersburg, FL
- Los Angeles Museum of the Holocaust, Los Angeles, CA
- New England Holocaust Memorial, Boston, MA
- Simon Wiesenthal Center, Los Angeles, CA
- The Stuart S. Elenko Collection, Holocaust Museum & Studies Center, Bronx High School of Science, New York, NY
- Virginia Holocaust Museum, Richmond, VA
- Zell Holocaust Memorial, Spertus Museum, Chicago, IL

Holocaust Memorials

Holocaust Remembrance Day
"Remember us."

Holocaust survivors report these were often the last words of victims as they were marched to their deaths in the **gas chambers.**

In 1951, the Israeli government passed a law that provided for a Yom Hashoah, or Holocaust Remembrance Day. This commemoration was to take place each year on the 27th Nissan of the Hebrew calendar, a date that usually falls towards the end of April or the beginning of May. Among the most moving of the annual ceremonies held at Yad Vashem, Israel's Holocaust memorial, is a tribute called "Unto Every Person There is a Name."

Members of the public are invited to stand in the sacred Hall of Remembrance and read out the names of Jewish Holocaust victims.

Remembrance Day is meant not only as a time to mourn the dead. It is a time to think about what could have been done to save them. The Holocaust could have been prevented. Again and again governments and individuals throughout the sad history of 1939–1945 could have saved innocent people had bold steps been taken.

Before September of 1939, when the killing began, Hitler had offered to send Germany's Jews to the United States, Canada, Great Britain, and other countries. No country was willing to accept the hardship of taking the thousands and thousands of new immigrants.

Memories of Courage

The history of the Holocaust is more than indifference, destruction, and loss. It is also about survival, resistance, and courage. In the face of cruelty and danger, some people refused to be bystanders and acted—often paying with their lives.

They affirmed life and honored humanity.

To learn about these heroes and Days of Remembrance, visit the Museum's Web site at www.ushmm.org

NATIONAL DAYS OF REMEMBRANCE

April 8–15, 2002

100 Raoul Wallenberg Place, SW, Washington, DC 20024-2126; (202) 488-0400

UNITED STATES HOLOCAUST MEMORIAL MUSEUM

Remembering Those Lost

Yom Hashoah was made a national public holiday in Israel in 1959. Many people celebrate with candlelighting, speakers, poems, prayers, and singing. Some people read from a list of Holocaust victims in order to gain the significance of the six million Jews lost.

Debate continues today regarding U.S. war planners' decisions not to bomb the railroad tracks leading to Auschwitz in 1944. By then, reliable reports of what was going on there had been received by U.S. officials. It was decided that diverting military resources to a target that would not directly help win the war might delay Hitler's defeat. In the meantime, trainloads of victims and supplies continued to arrive at the gates of the killing factory even as the **Nazis** were losing the war.

Yad Vashem: Israel's Memorial

Yad Vashem, the Holocaust Martyrs' and Heroes' Remembrance Authority, was created in Israel in 1953. Yad Vashem covers 45 acres (18 hectares) of Har Hazikaron, the Mount of Remembrance.

The memorial's Hall of Remembrance is a quiet, darkened room with a high ceiling that rises to a small skylight. The names of the six **death camps** and some of the **concentration camps** and killing sites throughout Europe are etched into the stone floor. In front of a memorial flame, a crypt holds the ashes of some of the victims.

The nearby Childrens' Memorial, a tribute to the one and a half million children who died as a result of the Holocaust, is built into an underground cave. Burning candles, a traditional Jewish memorial to the dead, fill the darkness.

The Valley of Communities is a 2 1/2-acre (1-hectare) monument of high stone walls dug out of Israel's bedrock. Engraved on each wall are the names of some of the more than five thousand Jewish communities destroyed or made to suffer under the Nazis.

The Memorial to the Deportees is one of the actual cattle cars used to transport thousands of Jews to concentration camps. The car is perched on the edge of a cliff facing the Jerusalem forest. The cliff is meant to symbolize the coming horror these people faced, while the forest represents rebirth in the state of Israel.

Among the memorials are two offering hope for the world. The Avenue and Garden of the Righteous Among the Nations honor non-Jews who "acted according to the most noble principles of humanity and risked their lives to help Jews during the Holocaust." Here, Israelis have planted two thousand trees, each bearing the name of one brave non-Jewish person who stood against **Nazi** terror. The names of other heroic people called "Righteous Among the Nations," are engraved on the walls of the Garden of the Righteous Among the Nations. The memories of 150,000 people from many different nations are celebrated in this way.

The Berlin Memorial

On October 31, 2001, after ten years of debate and planning, German parliament president Wolfgang Thierse climbed up into a power shovel and removed the ceremonial first scoopful of dirt from a building site near Berlin's famous Brandenburg Gate. Here would stand Germany's national memorial to the victims of Nazi crimes. "We have an obligation to keep alive the memory of what crimes mankind is capable of," he said. "Not to spread a guilt complex but to encourage responsibility."

Writer Lea Rosh first proposed a memorial in 1988. "I wouldn't have thought it would take so long and I also wouldn't have thought it would be so difficult," she said.

"The lively debates about its building and the form it would take were part of a process of understanding how to deal with our past," Wolfgang Thierse said.

Dr. Yanush Korczak

This statue of Yanush Korczak and his children is at Yad Vashem. Yanush was an educator and leader of the Warsaw Orphanage in Poland. He was given the chance to leave his children behind and escape the Nazis. Yanush decided to stay with the children. He, along with his children, were killed at Treblinka camp.

Eisenman's Plan

Just as important as Peter Eisenman's design is the location of the memorial. The Berlin Holocaust Memorial will lie between the Brandenburg Gate and the bunker where Adolf Hitler died.

The controversial design for the memorial by American architect Peter Eisenman was the winner of an international competition. The monument will cover more than 20,000 square feet (2,000 square meters). Twenty-seven hundred plain concrete slabs of differing heights will be lined up in rows across an open space slightly below street level. Eisenman intended to symbolically portray the relentless order with which the Nazis exterminated Europe's Jews. Some thought the design should have been less abstract—perhaps containing statues of victims and other human elements—others felt the monument should not occupy such a central part of Berlin.

Plans are to have the Berlin Holocaust Memorial completed by January 27, 2004, the 59th anniversary of the **liberation** of the Auschwitz-Birkenau **concentration camp.**

Holocaust Education

The Holocaust did not have to happen. It took place in large part because too many good people failed to stand up and strongly reject Hitler's ideas. In this spirit, the United States Holocaust Memorial Museum sponsors many educational programs.

Every summer, students from around the United States meet with peers from Germany, Luxembourg, and Washington, D.C. Together they learn about the implications of the Holocaust in their own lives today. They discuss what role the world's democracies can play in preventing such things from happening again. Other programs teach about the U.S. Holocaust Memorial Museum itself and how to study the history of the Holocaust. Another program helps students learn how to ask the right questions about historical objects and photographs from the Holocaust.

The March of the Living

Every year, teenagers from around the world gather in Poland and Israel and retrace the history of the Holocaust for themselves. They begin by seeing where Jewish communities once flourished in cities like Warsaw, Kraków, and Lublin. The group then makes a much more difficult journey. They travel to Auschwitz-Birkenau, Treblinka, and other **concentration camps** and try to comprehend what took place there.

On Holocaust Remembrance Day each year, participants go on a March of the Living. Young people from all over the world, most of them Jews, walk shoulder-to-shoulder from Auschwitz concentration camp to the Birkenau killing center. What was a march of death for so many innocent people becomes a memorial service and a hopeful promise never to forget them.

The second leg of the journey addresses the arrival of tens of thousands of survivors and their families in Israel in the years following **liberation** from the camps. Current problems in the Middle East and the complex peace process are discussed.

Children's Programs

A volunteer speaks to a school group in front of the children's tile wall in the Gonda Education Center at the U.S. Holocaust Memorial Museum.

Fighting the Lies

Education becomes vitally important in battling hatred. Various individuals and groups throughout the world believe that Hitler was a great leader. These **Nazis** and Nazi sympathizers often attempt to argue that the Holocaust either never took place or has been exaggerated. They employ false evidence, or twist facts to promote their hateful ideas.

Other Holocaust deniers use Nazi records and written plans to argue that no systematic attempt to kill Jews existed. Nazi authorities were usually careful to write in code when discussing procedures at the **death camps**—referring to people and corpses as "pieces," for instance. Because these documents rarely directly discuss the killing of people and the disposal of human remains, Holocaust deniers claim Jews were not murdered but died of **typhus** and other diseases.

A number of organizations have dedicated themselves to making sure these seeds of hatred are never given a chance to grow. The Simon Wiesenthal Center and the Jewish Anti-defamation League are just two prominent "watchdog" groups that monitor the activities of hate groups. Such groups do everything from posting rebuttals to pro-Nazi **propaganda** in Internet chat rooms, to notifying police

The Living March On

These people are beginning the March of the Living. From Auschwitz, they will walk toward Birkenau, to commemorate the people who walked this path to their deaths during the Holocaust.

and government officials when hate groups threaten violent action, to providing educational anti-hatred seminars at local schools.

The Role of the Internet

The danger of the Internet is that groups and individuals can spread hateful messages with relative ease. The Nizkor Project is one of several organizations dedicated to standing up to anyone who denies the Holocaust occurred. The Nizkor Project offers Holocaust research guides, information about the camps, details from the Nuremberg Trials, biographies of people involved in the Holocaust, and other useful information pertaining to the Holocaust.

What do German Young People Learn?

Every country has made mistakes. Most have shameful episodes in their histories. But few countries carry the burden of guilt born by Germany. For many in the world, the Holocaust and Adolf Hitler are the first thoughts that come to mind when Germany is mentioned.

Teaching children about the Holocaust is difficult in Germany. Words and activities must be carefully chosen so students do not feel as if they are supposed to feel guilty about what happened. Many German schoolchildren are taken on field trips to **concentration camps.**

Germany Today

Today's German government has made it illegal to lie about the Holocaust. Holocaust deniers are prosecuted. How do Germans your age feel about the Holocaust? The events took place during the time of their grandparents. Some feel guilty and embarrassed to be German. Others feel angry that the world still sees them as being somehow responsible for crimes committed long before they were even born.

Too Much Guilt?

By the time German students reach the age of ten, most have spent a good deal of time studying World War II and the Holocaust. Because denying the Holocaust took place is a crime, few students doubt the facts. There are, however, young people who reject what they learn in school. They are fascinated with Adolf Hitler and the past.

This rise of young **"neo-Nazis"** concerns many German teachers. During 2001, these so-called "skinheads" were responsible for a number of deadly attacks on foreigners and **synagogues.** "The fact that we can't look back on the last century with any pride is certainly difficult for some young people," says Anita Maechler, a teacher in Berlin. "Kids want to be proud of something and need to identify with something."

Nazism in the same way one can give a child an immunization shot to prevent the flu. "The preparation is crucial. It must be clear to them that this is a place for which they bear no personal responsibility in the sense of guilt. Such ideas must be broken down in advance and that's not always the case."

Dr. Guenther Morsch, head of the museum at Sachsenhausen camp, worries that too many German educators believe you can simply take a group of students on a tour of a concentration camp and they will be prevented from believing pro-**Nazi** messages. Showing German children the horrors that are part of their history, he argues, will not "immunize" them against

Just as the children and grandchildren of survivors are still haunted by the events of the 1940s, so German teenagers continue to grieve over what the Nazi's did. Some may even wonder about a grandfather's or a grandmother's role in those dark days. German schools continue to search for the best ways to deal with this legacy.

What We're Still Finding Out

We still do not know all there is to know about the Holocaust. New stories are still being discovered. In 2001, for example, a historian and journalist named Jan Gross uncovered and publicized the truth about a massacre that had remained virtually unknown for 60 years. In the town of Jedwabne in Poland, a monument declared that on July 10, 1941, Germans troops forced 1,600 of Jedwabne's Jewish citizens into a barn and burned them alive. Through his research, Gross revealed that the killers were not Germans. They were Poles, the neighbors and fellow citizens of the victims.

It turns out that on that day, even the **Nazis** were shocked by the brutality of the locals who participated. Once the adults were burned alive in the barn, the murderers found all the Jewish children who were hiding. They tied the children together and used pitchforks to throw them onto the burning embers of the barn.

A New Look at Polish Anti-Semitism

This historical detective work has shaken the vision many Polish people had of their country. Most saw themselves only as victims of the Nazis, never as collaborators. Now, Poland's Institute of National Remembrance has been given the job of determining exactly what happened in Jedwabne and similar towns where other such massacres took place.

Hitler's Willing Executioners?

In 1999, scholar Daniel Jonah Goldhagen released a book titled *Hitler's Willing Executioners: Ordinary Germans and the Holocaust.* In the book, Goldhagen argued that a huge number of German citizens were willing and often enthusiastic participants in murder and torture.

Goldhagen believes that centuries of widely-accepted German **anti-Semitism**

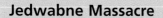

Jedwabne Massacre

These photos show a few of the victims of the Jedwabne massacre. Some of the killers were brought to justice. In a 1949 trial, twelve Jedwabne men were sentenced to prison terms and one, Karol Bardon, who was named as the leader, was sentenced to death. The sentence was never carried out.

A Monumental Court Battle

The trial between Irving and Lipstadt represented a huge victory for scholars and historians who stand up against Holocaust deniers. In effect, the court ruled that the Holocaust happened. Thus, to call someone who claims it did not a liar is an accurate statement, not simply a matter of opinion.

David Irving

Deborah Lipstadt

led to their participation in the Holocaust. He argues against the idea that only the special forces of the **SS** participated in massacres and organized cruelty. In fact, many ordinary German soldiers turned into vicious participants in atrocities while in Russia and Poland. He describes many instances of German police or citizens without criminal backgrounds participating in the murder of Jews without being threatened by Nazi authorities. His controversial argument that ordinary Germans—rather than a small group of bad people—helped Adolf Hitler and the Nazis carry out **genocide** created new debate over who or what deserved blame for the Holocaust.

Fighting for the Truth

Recently, a huge legal victory was won by historians defending the world's memory of the Holocaust. In England, a scholar named Deborah Lipstadt had been sued by a British Holocaust denier named David Irving. Lipstadt wrote a book about Holocaust deniers in which she called Irving, "[o]ne of the most dangerous spokespersons for Holocaust denial."

Irving was a favorite of groups and individuals denying the Holocaust because, in addition to his activities as a Holocaust denier, he had written several respected histories of World War II.

The lawsuit became a worldwide event. Under British law, Lipstadt and the publishing house of Penguin Books were required to prove that the Holocaust had really happened in order to prove claims Irving twisted the truth were not "libelous." To libel someone is to unfairly damage their reputation.

The judge in the case was blunt in stating that based on the mass of evidence presented at the trial "no objective, fair-minded historian would have serious cause to doubt that there were **gas chambers** at Auschwitz, and that they were operated on a substantial scale to kill hundreds of thousands of Jews." Further, the judge concluded that to call Mr. Irving "dangerous" was justified by his anti-Semitic views and use of falsified history to promote them.

Legacy of the Holocaust

In 1948, the **United Nations** held the Convention on the Prevention and Punishment of the Crime of **Genocide.** Under an agreement ratified there, the United States and most of the world's countries vowed to "undertake, to prevent, and to punish" the crime of genocide.

However, the agreement has not prevented genocide, nor has it brought justice down on those who have committed such crimes. It has proven extremely difficult to stop events taking place on the soil of far-off countries. The sort of people who would commit genocide do not always heed strong words or laws.

Further, when words fail to make murderers cease the slaughter, the nations of the world often have trouble coming to an agreement on what is to be done quickly enough to be effective. In some cases corrupt, non-democratic governments can only be made to stop committing crimes through military action. To send United States military personnel into harm's way is always a difficult decision for leaders. In cases where the lives and property of Americans are not directly effected, the decision is even harder to make.

Because of such concerns, help is often slow in coming. Mass killings and other atrocities committed against Muslims in Yugoslavia, as well as endless pictures of civilians dodging sniper bullets in Sarajevo, finally pushed the United States to direct action. Sustained U.S. bombing led to Serbian military defeats. Serb leader Slobodan Milosevic finally agreed to stop Serbian aggression. But it had taken the murder and rape of hundreds of thousands of Muslims beginning three years earlier to bring U.S. forces into the picture. Today, Milosevic and some of his aides and commanders face a **War Crimes Tribunal** that could sentence them to up to life in prison.

Without a Home

Thousands of Tutsis were forced into refugee camps in Rwanda. Most times, all they had were the clothes on their backs.

Other times, help has failed to arrive at all. In 1994, reports out of Rwanda, a small country in Central Africa, confirmed that members of the Hutu tribe had begun killing their Tutsi neighbors. Of the country's seven million people, about 90% were Hutu.

Encouraged by hateful radio broadcasts by Hutu extremists, Hutus armed with machetes and rifles slaughtered every Tutsi they could find. Meanwhile, the United Nations was slow to act. During the days of terror, the U.N. and the U.S. government took great pains to avoid calling the event a genocide. Acknowledging a genocide would mean they become obligated by the Convention on the Prevention and Punishment of the Crime of Genocide to send in troops to stop the killing. Again, a decision to put U.S. troops in danger where U.S. citizens are not directly threatened is nearly always a last resort.

In addition to the continued danger of genocide, Europe remains threatened by the rise of **right-wing** politicians who wish to drive foreigners out. In 1999, Austrians voted Joerg Haider and his Freedom Party a big share of power in the government. Many of Haider's followers have a long history of **anti-Semitism** and argue that foreigners have been the cause of much of Austria's economic troubles. The world reacted with alarm to these election results. On February 1, 2000, Haider's Freedom Party announced they were joining with another, less extreme party to lead the Austrian government. Germany has experienced increasing attacks on foreigners by **neo-Nazi** teenagers.

Hatred between Jews and Muslims leads to fighting and murder almost daily in Israel and the Palestinian-controlled Gaza Strip. In the eyes of many Muslims throughout the world, the state of Israel's military

41

power and its willingness to use force has changed Jews from victims to oppressors. Those who defend Israel's actions point out that because some Palestinians and all Islamic terrorists resort to violence and wish to destroy Israel, they must be dealt with harshly.

Disco in Auschwitz?

Auschwitz was the German name for the Polish town Oswiecim. In August of 2000, Polish investors got permission to open a **discotheque** there. The problem was that the disco was to be located in a former tannery where Holocaust victims worked and died. Much of the world sees the entire area of the Auschwitz-Birkenau camp as a huge burial ground. A disco placed there becomes, for them, an invitation to dance on the graves of the murdered. Strong protests from various groups led to the closing of the disco. Plans for a shopping center nearby are going ahead however.

Many Jews were upset about how the Auschwitz site was being treated before the arrival of these businesses. The Catholic diocese of Poland has turned the camp's former **SS** headquarters into a church. **Rabbi** Avi Weiss, president of the Coalition for Jewish Concerns-Amcha, claims the church is a desecration of sacred Jewish ground:

> *The disco and shopping center are horrors, but the greatest violation of the memory of six million is the church at Birkenau. It was from the S.S. headquarters, now the church, that the orders to exterminate were given, where Jewish women were raped and murdered... [Protesters] have been accused of being anti-Catholic but that's simply not true. We have a deep respect for all beliefs. But we take exception to a church being placed in the largest Jewish cemetery in the world.*

Such emotional debates will continue. The crimes committed in Oswiecim have ended forever its chance to be a normal city. The sadness and destruction brought by Hitler's **Final Solution** will never disappear from the towns and villages where it was nearly carried out.

The "System"

Polish teens dance at the disco in Oswiecim, Poland, called the "System." It closed shortly after opening in 2000.

A History of Genocide

The Holocaust was an event unprecedented in the number of people murdered and the factory-like methods used to kill them. But the history of the world is blackened by many **genocidal** events. Here are a few genocides committed during the 20th century:

1904–1905	The Herero people of southwest Africa are destroyed by German settlers and the German army.
1915–1916	The Turks massacre one million Armenians.
1937–1938	Japanese soldiers commit "The Rape of Nanking," brutally murdering 300,000 Chinese and committing countless atrocities.
1965–1966	The Indonesian army kills as many as one million **Communists** and their families.
1972	Pakistan's army murders between one million and three million Bengalis.
1972	In Burundi, 100,000 to 150,000 Hutus are massacred by the ruling Tutsis.
1975–1979	Two million Cambodians are slaughtered by the Khmer Rouge of Kampuchea.
1975–present	In East Timor, more than 200,000 islanders who desire independence have been killed by the Indonesian army. Indians in Brazil, Guatemala, and other parts of South America have been targeted and killed in huge numbers by government forces.
1992–1995	Two hundred thousand Muslims are murdered during the "ethnic cleansing" of Yugoslavia by Serbian forces.
1994	Eight hundred thousand Tutsis are murdered by Hutus in Rwanda.

The Committee on Conscience, an organization dedicated to the prevention of genocide, warns that Sudan may be the site of the next genocide. The Sudanese government is attempting to move the Dinka, Nuer, and Nuba peoples off of land that holds valuable oil. Two million people have already died and four million have been displaced during a terrible seventeen-year civil war.

Liz and Jakob Liwazer

Liz Liwazer grew up in West Bloomfield, Michigan, a suburb of Detroit. The town is home to a large Jewish population and a number of Holocaust survivors. Liz's father, Jakob, is one of them. For Jakob, raising a family was "one way to get revenge against Hitler. Throughout history, at various times they have tried to get rid of the Jews and have always failed. To have a beautiful family meant the **Nazis** failed, too."

Along with building a family, Jakob decided he would try not to think about what happened to him while in Dachau **concentration camp** and on a death march. He was, he says, "looking always to the future, to building a life in the United States. To going forward." He remained silent about all he'd seen and experienced for 51 years, until 1996.

That year, at Liz's urging, Jakob testified as part of the Shoah Foundation's effort to videotape the stories of all living survivors and witnesses. He had never told his three daughters all he had suffered. "Before the Shoah interview, I only had very sketchy details," Liz says. "He could talk about pre-war Poland then suddenly it was always 1950 and he was in New York."

Jakob wanted to shield his children from the things he suffered as a young man. The story of his life in the dark years between were a secret Jakob shared with no one. Liz recalls:

I knew that he was in a concentration camp and on a death march but I wasn't sure exactly where. He would talk about his life in Warsaw before the war—he came from a very wealthy family and he would talk about the country home he would go to with his eight brothers and sisters.

Father and Daughter

This picture of Jakob and Liz Liwazer was taken in West Bloomfield, Michigan, in January 1997. Family and friends had come together to celebrate Jakob's granddaughter's first Sabbath dinner.

Only three of the nine Liwazer children survived the war, the oldest having left in 1935 for Palestine, now the state of Israel. While growing up, Liz never wanted to burden her father by forcing him to talk about a past she knew was too painful to revisit. But her mind often spun its own nightmares and she worried about him. The profound grief she knew he carried effected her, too.

Liz remembers that her father, despite his bad memories, always tried to focus on the positive in his life and in his story:

*The most detail he ever gave us was about how the American soldiers **liberated** him when he was on the death march. He commemorates May 2 as the day he was freed. He talked about how the soldiers threw chocolates and cigarettes to these starving people, that they didn't know what to expect and were clearly shocked to see the condition of the survivors.*

His story remained hidden, but it had shaped her father's view of the world in ways that were obvious as she grew up.

My dad was always overprotective of us—and very, very fearful. For example, when we got our driver's licenses, we had to have much more [driving] experience than anyone else, and then when we finally did get them [licenses], he still wouldn't let us drive in the dark.

Liz and her father have a very close relationship. Each worries a lot about the other. Jakob wants to protect Liz from danger and wants to know she is safe at all times. "If my flight is delayed or something else delays me in reassuring

A Family Wedding

Jakob's sister Fela was married in Warsaw, Poland, in 1938. Pictured here are (seated, from left) Edzia (sister), Marek Przeworski (groom), Elzunia (Edzia's daughter), Fela (sister, bride), Mrs. Przeworski (groom's mother). Top row (from left) are Liza (sister), Jakob, Ben-Zion (father), grandmother (father's mother), unidentified young

man, unidentified cousin, Justina Finkelstein (cousin), Adasz (brother), unidentified cousin. Not all of Jakob's immediate family are present. Missing are his sisters, Dyna and Frania, and his brothers, Julek and Mietek.

him I'm safe and sound, he gets very anxious and tells me how he was 'on pins and needles' waiting to hear from me." Of course, all parents worry about their children. But the emotions involved are stronger when you know your father has lost so many people in his life. So Liz worries that her father is worrying.

> I'm always very careful not to give my dad more things to worry about. He doesn't know that I traveled to Guatemala, even though I was a 30-year-old woman at the time. When I went on a five-week road trip this summer across the country—kind of a dream of mine—I couldn't tell him because he would worry so much. In contrast, when I told my sister not to tell him she said: 'You're 36 years old!'

When the Shoah Foundation put out a call requesting survivors provide videotaped testimony, Liz decided it was time to push her father to answer all the questions. At first he was reluctant. The foundation had already gathered stories from 10,000 people. Jakob said that they had enough and did not need his. "He was very reluctant—even though he had talked about writing his experiences, or that I would write his story."

Things changed when Jakob learned that his sister Liza had been interviewed and video-taped. When Jakob saw her taped testimony, Liz remembers, he was critical. He felt his sister had left out important historical details. He would "do it right." "This happened around his 83rd birthday," Liz recalls. "This really shows you that sibling rivalry can play out at any age!"

Jakob says that, sibling rivalries aside, what changed his mind was his feeling of

Liberated!

Upon **liberation,** Jakob was issued an identification card at a **displaced persons camp** in Munich, Germany. The card shows that Jakob had been imprisoned in **ghettos** and **concentration camps** from August 25, 1941 until May 2, 1945. In the picture he still wears the familiar striped coat of his concentration camp uniform.

CERTIFICATE
Nr. 109

The jewish ex-prisoner of the Dachau concentration-camp
Liwaser Jakob
(name)
Ex-prisiner Nr. 91998
born 19. II. 1914 at Warsaw
(Date) (place)
last domicile
(full adress)
was kept in Nazi-german concetration-camps
from 25. VIII 1941 to 2. V 1945
and was liberated by allied troops.

The Jewish Committee   Camp's commandant
Director UNRRA

Munich, 4 / VII   1945

Registered at D. P. Center Nr. 2
Munich-Freimann (Flakkaserne) on
1945
The Jewish Committee

Owner's signature

Surviving the Worst

Jakob stands with two friends from his time in the ghetto and the camp—brothers Mischa and Abraham Slezin—in March 1947. Jakob, Mischa, and Abraham survived the Shaulai Ghetto in Lithuania, as well as Dachau concentration camp. Jakob shared his meager ration of bread with one of the brothers, who never forgot this sacrifice.

responsibility to the memory of his family and his belief in the need for people to know about exactly what happened. "Young people must know the history or it will repeat," he says.

When asked whether the experience of telling his story for three hours after so many years of silence changed his life, he thinks for a moment. "I am glad I did it because it was the right thing to do. I am grateful to Steven Spielberg because now future generations will be able to hear a voice, see a face, and always remember."

When Liz finally viewed her father's video-taped testimony—family members are not present during the interview—it was an emotional experience. She cried all day.

"I kind of resented that the interviewer and cameraman knew the details of my dad's life before I did," she adds. This was likely true for thousands of the children of survivors who provided testimony after more than 50 years of silence. "He thanked me in the end for pursuing it," Liz says. "I think going through the experience of talking about that time in his life for three hours in front of a video camera liberated him in terms of no longer having to shield us from those horrors."

Jakob has also begun visiting schools to tell students about the Holocaust. "Such education is essential," he says. The reaction of students lets him know what he's told them is important to them. Many ask to shake his hand.

Jakob feels that since he was lucky and strong enough to survive, he must make his life worthwhile in honor of those who did not. He works on behalf of many charitable organizations, especially those that focus on education. Liz says that when groups try to honor him for his contributions of time, money, and effort, he declines. "I'm not doing these things for that reason," he says.

Liz says that she, too, feels special pressure to make her life worthwhile. "After all my

47

Helping Others

After the war, Jakob helped displaced people find their families. In this picture, Jakob (right) and his cousin, Chaplain Lt. Colonel Hirsch Liwazer (left) help with a Munich transport of displaced people to Marseille, France en route to Israel. Also above are the papers he needed in order to help with the transports.

father went through to survive and build a family... there is a lot of pressure to live a meaningful life."

The terrorist attacks of September 11, 2001, were especially upsetting for Jakob. It was a reminder that violence motivated by hatred can reach the United States. The United States strongly supports Israel and thus is a target of Islamic terrorists who wish to destroy the Jewish state. But he tries to remain positive even about these events: "love is such a powerful thing," he says. "What you saw in those [World Trade Center] towers is that when faced with death, people called their loved ones to tell them they loved them. And strangers held

hands together as they died. It shows how people need each other and need to be together and that's the good thing that can come out of disaster—that love is more powerful."

In the end, the **Nazis** could not achieve destruction of the Jews because of love. Having lived through as terrible a time as the world has ever known, Jakob's response was not to seek some sort of violent and hateful revenge. He tells of how he came to the United States with one goal: to rebuild his life by creating his "beautiful family." His Jewish children and grandchildren become his answer to Adolf Hitler's hatred.

The Liwazer Family Today

Jakob Liwazer is the proud father and grandfather of a beautiful family. His family is just one example of how Holocaust survivors have prevailed over this dark time in history. Through his family, Jakob has not only passed on his religious beliefs, but also his example of how love can always triumph over hatred in the end.

Front row, from left: Avi Beneson (grandson); Liz Liwazer (daughter); Anita Blender (daughter); Abbey Blender (granddaughter)

Middle row, from left: David Beneson (son-in-law); Jakob Liwazer; Dennis Blender (son-in-law); Katie Blender (granddaughter)

Back row, from left: Jeana Beneson (granddaughter); Marci Beneson (daughter); Vicki Beneson (granddaughter); Esther Liwazer (wife)

Timeline

1933	
January 30	Hitler comes to power in Germany as Chancellor.
February 27	A fire breaks out at the *Reichstag*, the German Parliament. The **Nazis** blame the **Communists** and produce a Dutch Communist who confesses.
February 28	German President Hindenburg's decree, "For the Protection of the People and the State," allows for the creation of **concentration camps.** The Nazis persuade Hindenburg to pass the decree to fight what they called the "Communist threat" after the fire at the *Reichstag.*
March 5	New elections are held. The Nazis win easily with intimidation.
March 17	The **SS** (short for "*Schutzstaffel,*" security staff) is set up as Hitler's bodyguard.
March 21	Dachau, the first Nazi concentration camp is set up. Concentration camps and **labor camps** are set up steadily after this.
April 1	Jewish stores in Berlin are boycotted.
May 10	Books written by Jews and Nazi opponents are burned.

1934	
August 2	Hitler makes himself *Führer*, sole leader of Germany.

1935	
September 15	The Nuremberg Laws are passed against German Jews.

1936	
	Jewish doctors and dentists cannot work in state hospitals. Jews cannot become judges, join the army, or work in the book trade.

1937	
	Jewish businesses are **"Aryanized."**

1938	
March 13	Germany takes over Austria.
March 15	The German army marches into Prague, Czechoslovakia.
November 9	**Synagogues** are burned and Jewish stores and homes are looted in *Kristallnacht.*

1939	
March 15	Germany takes control of all of Czechoslovakia.
September 1	Germany invades Poland and takes immediate action against Polish Jews.
September 3	Britain and France declare war on Germany.

1940	
April 9	Germany invades Denmark and Norway.
April 30	The Nazis set up the Lodz **Ghetto** in Poland.
May 10	Germany invades Belgium, France, Luxembourg, and Holland.

1941	
April 6	Germany invades Yugoslavia and Greece.
June 22	Germany invades the Soviet Union and begins killing Jews in large numbers.
From September	Mass gassings at Auschwitz begin with Soviet **prisoners-of-war** and continue. They focus on Jews and become more regular from January 1942 on.
October 10	Terezín Ghetto is set up in Czechoslovakia.
December 7	Japan bombs Pearl Harbor.
December 8	The first group of Jews are gassed at Chelmo **death camp** in Poland.
December 11	Germany declares war on the United States.

1942	
January 20	The Wannsee Conference is called to discuss the **"Final Solution"** to the "Jewish Problem."

1943	
June 11	Heinrich Himmler orders all remaining ghettos to be emptied and their inhabitants killed.

1944	
From June	Death marches (called this because so many of the prisoners on the marches died while marching) from camps in Poland begin. Prisoners are marched westward, in front of advancing Soviet troops.
June 6	Allied troops land in Normandy, France.
August 4	Anne Frank and her family are arrested in Amsterdam.
1945	
April 30	Hitler commits suicide in Berlin.
May 7	Germany surrenders to the Allies.
November	The Nuremberg trials of Nazi war criminals begin. The first war criminals are executed in October 1946.
1947	
	Anne Frank's diary is first published.
1953	
	Yad Vashem, the Holocaust Martyrs' and Heroes' Remembrance Authority, is created in Israel.
1958	
	Elie Wiesel writes *Night*. It is first released in English in 1960.
1959	
	Yom Hashoah, or Holocaust Remembrance Day, becomes a national public holiday in Israel.
1985	
	Claude Lanzmann releases his nine-hour documentary, *Shoah*.
1986	
	Art Spiegelman writes and draws *Maus I: My Father Bleeds History*.
1991	
	Art Spiegelman writes and draws *Maus II: And Here My Troubles Began*.
1992	
	Art Spiegelman wins the Pulitzer Prize for *Maus*.
1993	
	Steven Spielberg releases *Schindler's List*.
April 23	The United States Holocaust Memorial Museum opens in Washington, D.C.
1994	
	Schindler's List wins Academy Awards for Best Art Direction-Set Decoration; Best Cinematography; Best Director; Best Film Editing; Best Music, Original Score; Best Picture; and Best Writing, Screenplay Based on Material from Another Medium.
	Steven Spielberg establishes the Survivors of the Shoah Visual History Foundation.
	The French government establishes The Musee Memorial des Enfants d'Izieu.
1997	
	Hector Feliciano writes his book, *The Lost Museum: The Nazi Conspiracy to Steal the World's Greatest Works of Art*.
1998	
	Roberto Benigni releases *Life is Beautiful*.
1999	
	Daniel Jonah Goldhagen writes his book, *Hitler's Willing Executioners: Ordinary Germans and the Holocaust*.
	Life is Beautiful wins Academy Awards for Best Actor in a Leading Role; Best Foreign Language Film; and Best Music, Original Dramatic Score.
2000	
	Court case between David Irving and Deborah Lipstadt ends . The court rules that the Holocaust did happen.
2001	
	Olevano, a painting by Alexander Kanoldt, is returned to the family of Dr. Ismar Littman.
	Daniel Barenboim conducts a piece by Richard Wagner, an **anti-Semite**, in Jerusalem.
October 31	Ground is broken in Berlin, Germany, for the Berlin Holocaust Memorial.

Glossary

Allied Force name given to countries united to fight Germany and Japan in World War II. The Allies included the United States, Great Britain, and the Soviet Union.

anti-Semitism being prejudiced against Jewish people

Aryan word used by the Nazis to mean people with northern European ancestors, without any ancestors from what they called "inferior" races, such as Poles, Slavs, or Jews. Aryans were usually blonde, blue-eyed, and sturdy.

Communist person who believes that a country should be governed by the people of that country for the good of everyone in it. They believe private property is wrong, including owning a home or a business. The state should own everything and run everything, giving the people the things they need.

concentration camp prison camp set up by the Nazis under a special law that meant that the prisoners were never tried and were never given a release date. The Nazis could put anyone in these camps, for any reason or none, for as long as they wanted.

crematorium place with special ovens for burning bodies

cyanide highly poisonous chemical with industrial uses. The Nazis used cyanide in gas form to kill large groups of people in gas chambers.

death camp camp set up by the Nazis to murder as many people, most of them Jewish, as quickly and cheaply as possible. Most of the victims were gassed.

dictator leader with absolute power over a country

discotheque place where music is played for dancing and entertainment

displaced persons camp camp set up after World War II for people who had been taken from their homes and countries and separated from their families. Workers in these camps tried to trace families and help people return home.

Einsatzgruppen special unit of the German army set up by the Nazis. These units went into Eastern Europe at the same time as the army. Their job was supposedly to round up and kill civilians who were a danger to the Reich. In fact, they were told to kill Jews.

emigrate to leave one's country and settle in another

Final Solution Nazi plan to end Germany's so-called "Jewish Problem," by means of killing all Jews

gas chamber large room, often disguised as showers, that the Nazis filled with people. When the room was full the Nazis pumped gas into it, to kill the people inside.

genocide to kill or attempt to kill an entire group of people

Gestapo secret police set up by the Nazis in 1933. Agents of the Gestapo searched for Jews and other enemies of the Nazis for purposes of arrest and deportation to concentration camps.

ghetto area of a town or city, walled or fenced off from the rest of the city, where Jewish people were forced to live

gypsy member of a group of dark-skinned Europeans with roots in Romania and other Eastern European countries. Gypsies are known for choosing to move about in groups rather than settling in one place.

Jehovah's Witness religious group that was especially persecuted by the Nazis because members refused to swear an oath of loyalty to Hitler

labor camp camp set up by the Nazis that was a prison that used the prisoners as cheap labor

liberate used in this book to mean a place, especially a concentration camp, being freed from the control of the SS. Camps were liberated by Allied soldiers.

Luftwaffe German air force in World War II

munitions military weapons, ammunition, and supplies

Nazi member of the Nazi Party. Nazi is short for *Nationalsozialistische Deutsche Arbeiterpartei*, the National Socialist German Workers' Party.

neo-Nazi person who believes in and works to promote the principles of Adolf Hitler and the National Socialist Party today

prisoner of war soldier captured and held by the enemy

propaganda information and ideas that are worded and presented so that people will accept and believe them, even if they are not true

Protestant Christian who is in one of the churches that separated itself from the Catholic Church during the sixteenth century Reformation

rabbi Jewish scholar and spiritual leader. Rabbi means "teacher" in Hebrew.

right wing political party or portion of a political party opposed to Communism, Socialism, and other "progressive ideas" that would attempt to radically change society. Right-wing groups tend to promote traditional, old-fashioned values and range from Republicans in the United States to people like Adolf Hitler.

SS (short for *Schutzstaffel*) security staff. The SS began as Hitler's personal bodyguard. Later, they ran concentration camps and death camps. Everyone in the SS swore loyalty to Hitler, rather than Germany.

synagogue Jewish place of worship, the equivalent of a church or mosque

typhus disease caused by dirty conditions and spread by polluted water, usually polluted with sewage. Typhus causes high temperatures, rashes, vomiting, and diarrhea. It can be fatal.

undesirable word used by the Nazis to describe any person that they did not approve of because of political beliefs, race, religion, or behavior. Drug addicts and criminals are often called "undesirables" in the contemporary United States.

United Nations international organization dedicated to promoting world peace

War Crimes Tribunal established system for bringing to justice those accused of committing crimes during a war. A war crime is generally an act of brutality that goes beyond simply fighting a battle. The rape of women, intentional killing of civilians, and torture of captured soldiers are among the acts that would be called war crimes. A tribunal is a group of three judges that decides the guilt or innocence of the accused.

Further Reading

Frank, Anne. *Diary of a Young Girl.* Columbus, Ohio: Prentice Hall, 1993.

Shuter, Jane. *Auschwitz.* Chicago: Heinemann Library, 1999.

Tames, Richard. *Anne Frank.* Chicago: Heinemann Library, 1998.

Tames, Richard. *Adolf Hitler.* Chicago: Heinemann Library, 1998.

Whittock, Martyn. *Hitler & National Socialism.* Chicago: Heinemann Library, 1996.

Wiesel, Elie. *Night.* New York: Bantam Books, 1982.

Willoughby, Susan. *The Holocaust.* Chicago: Heinemann Library, 2000.

Sources

The author and publisher gratefully acknowledge the publications from which written sources in this book are drawn. In some cases, the wording or sentence structure has been simplified to make the material appropriate for a school readership.

Benigni, Roberto. "I wanted to make a beautiful movie: an interview with Roberto Benigni." By Enrika Milvy, from *http://www.salon.com,* 30 October 1998. (p. 20)

"Berlin Memorial Planned," *New York Times,* 18 January 1999, sec. A6. (p. 32)

"A Daughter's Hard Questions." *Newsweek* (24 January 2000): 50–51. (p. 10)

Dobrzynski, Judith. "A Bulldog on the Heels of Lost Nazi Loot," *New York Times,* 4 November 1997. (p. 15)

Evrony, Gila. From *http://web.wt.net/~gevro/st11.htm.* (pp. 9, 12)

Foxman, Abraham. "The Holocaust Meets Popular Culture," *New York Times,* 31 October 1998. (p. 16)

Israel Wire (6 October 2000). (p. 42)

Meyerowitz, Ruth. Interview by United States Holocaust Memorial Museum. In *http://www.ushmm.org.* (p. 10)

New York Times Magazine (3 December 1995): 75–80. (pp. 36, 37)

Oster, Shai. "Holocaust Humor." *Utne Reader* (September–October 1999): 86. (p. 8)

Pataki, Governor George E. From a press release (7 February 2001). In *http://www.state.ny.us/governor/press/year01/feb1_7_01.htm.* (p. 14)

Places of Interest and Websites

Florida Holocaust Museum
55 Fifth Street South
St. Petersburg, FL 33701
Visitor information: (727) 820-0100
Website: *http://www.flholocaustmuseum.org*

Holocaust Memorial Center
6602 West Maple Road
West Bloomfield, MI 48322
Visitor information: (248) 661-0840
Website: *http://holocaustcenter.org*

Holocaust Museum Houston
5401 Caroline Street
Houston, TX 77004
Visitor information: (713) 942-8000
Website: *http://www.hmh.org*

Simon Wiesenthal Center: Museum of Tolerance
Simon Wiesenthal Plaza
9786 West Pico Blvd.
Los Angeles, CA 90035
Visitor information: (310) 553-8403
Website: *http://www.museumoftolerance.com*

United States Holocaust Memorial Museum
100 Raoul Wallenberg Place, SW
Washington, D.C. 20024
Visitor information: (202) 488-0400
Website: *http://www.ushmm.org*

Website warning

1. Almost all Holocaust websites have been designed for adult users. They may contain horrifying and upsetting information and pictures.
2. Some people wish to minimize the Holocaust, or even deny that it happened at all. Some of their websites pretend to be delivering unbiased facts and information. To be sure of getting accurate information, it is always best to use an officially-recognized site, such as the ones listed on this page.
3. If you plan to visit a Holocaust website, ask an adult to view the site with you.

Index